Evernote

How to Use Evernote to Organize Your Day, Supercharge Your Life and Get More Done

Michael T. Robbins

D1605589

Published in The USA by:

Success Life Publishing

125 Thomas Burke Dr.

Hillsborough, NC 27278

Copyright © 2015 by Michael T. Robbins

ISBN-10: 151187077X

Disclaimer

Every effort has been made to accurately represent this book and its potential. Results vary with every individual, and your results may or may not be different from those depicted. No promises, guarantees or warranties, whether stated or implied, have been made that you will produce any specific result from this book. Your efforts are individual and unique, and may vary from those shown. Your success depends on your efforts, background and motivation.

The material in this publication is provided for educational and informational purposes only. Use of the programs, advice, and information contained in this book is at the sole choice and risk of the reader.

Table of Contents

An Introduction to Evernote

We live in a technologically advanced world where everything is in constant fast forward. The sad truth is that despite our technological advancements, our way of thinking has not changed much. What this means is that even with all the technology appliances at our disposal all aimed at making our lives easier, organized and productive, our lives are sometimes full of discord and disorganization.

As a personal organization enthusiast, I have found that one of the reasons why the technology at our disposal does not work well in streamlining our lives is the simple reason that we do not understand it nor bother to take the time to learn how to use and implement it in our lives properly.

Evernote is one of these technological advancements. If you ask anyone who has ever used Evernote and then gave it up along the way, he or she will tell you that their main reason is that they found developing the Evernote habit a bit tedious. This is despite the fact that using Evernote and developing the Evernote habit is relatively easy; all it requires is a bit of personal drive and some dedication. What does this mean?

It means that despite being fully aware of the effect Evernote has on organization and productivity, they did not feel bothered enough to implement the priceless values of Evernote to every pillar of their life. Before we get started in our organizational and productivity process using Evernote, I have to urge you; please implement Evernote to your organizational structure with an open mind. Implementing Evernote will create simple changes that have far-reaching effects in your daily life in terms of organization and productivity. This is the Evernote habit.

Let us kick off...

How Evernote Can Organize Your Life

Evernote is a digital, well-structured filing cabinet. With this said, I am sure you have heard of Evernote. If not, don't worry, within no time, you will be a pro at using it to streamline your life. Kindly allow me to ask you a question. If you had to guess or approximate, how many times have you used a paper napkin to write down a brilliant idea that hit you while you were on your lunch or coffee break? Be honest. For me (and this is before I discovered Evernote), at the end of each week, I could count 20-30 napkins (I am very creative).

Now, regardless of how meticulously organized we are, 20-30 napkins is no organizational joke. For me, this meant that in the course of the week, my computer screen would be beaded and decorated all-round the monitor frame with colorful sticky notes. Can you imagine how my computer monitor must have looked? Chaotic, disorganized, untidy, unproductive and whatever other negative energy words you can come up with would be the best description of what I was going through.

How many times do you get the urge and impulse to write down a genius idea only to find that your trusted paperback notebook and pen are nowhere in sight?

What if there was a way to make sure that those genius moments that always seem to come when you least expect them do not go uncaptured? What if there was a way you could make and organize all those sticky notes in one place without creating the clutter that comes with physical paper?

What if you could schedule your life and view it on multiple platforms at any time of day? What if you could create notes on your home computer and share them with colleagues instantly so that they can add their bit? Does this not sound like the embodiment of organization and productivity? To me, it does. Guess what the "what if's," we have mentioned above are possible. How? With Evernote! Regardless of what you do, who you are or what your organizational structure looks like, Evernote has something in store for you and can streamline almost every aspect of your life if you learn how to use and effectively implement what you have learned.

There is no shortage to reasons of why you should use this application to implement change in your life. Nevertheless, top on the list is organization and productivity. This to me is the crux of Evernote. There is also no disputing the fact that no matter who you are, Evernote has been tailor made for you.

What does this mean? It means that on top of the normal daily note taking we undertake every day, which we can port into Evernote rather than using the traditional notebook, there is still so much more you can do with the application. For the

stay-at-home mom, you can create recipes, and To-do lists; for the business executive, you can organize your hard copy digitally by scanning them using your smart device. This is not the end; whoever you are, you can organize files in accordance to a filing system that works for you by using tags and notebooks, which is what we shall look at shortly.

Now that we have a general understanding of Evernote, what it means to your organization and productivity, and have understood why we need it, take this chance to get the application before we move on to the next learning stages. To install the application on your computer, head over to the Evernote's homepage and download the most recent version of Evernote. Fortunately, Evernote identifies your platform and offers you the relevant file i.e. for Mac, Windows, or Ubuntu. Once the executable for windows completes downloading, install it, launch it, and create a free account by using an active email address and an easy to remember but secure password.

Using 'Notes' to De-Clutter the Chaos

Evernote's core functionality is the ability to create notes, as many as 100,000. How many sticky notes are these? Quite a lot I would guess. On a day-to-day basis, there are things we need to save, either for later referencing or as reminders. These files could be anything from a To-do list, a reminder, a simple note, a note with audio and pictures and even a note with attachments such as PDFs. Evernote makes all these functionalities possible.

In my many years of using Evernote (since I discovered it and stopped using sticky notes), I can honestly say that Evernote has performed miracles to my overall organization and in extension productivity. How so? This is all because I can save everything (files I use every day) as notes, which I can access easily on Evernote. Does this sound like something that could benefit your life? If so, let us look at creating your first note; this is the basic unit of all your "Evernoting" efforts or activities regardless of your field of work or study.

Before we move on, perhaps I should also mention that every file you save will fall into the note category. You can use the notes feature to store digital content, thoughts, ideas, reminders, and any other file you think is important as long as

it does not exceed 25MB (this is the maximum size of a single note if you are a free user).

How to create your first note in Evernote

To create your first note, start by launching your Evernote application. Go to file and select create new note (Figure 2 below). Evernote will create an "untitled note" that you can rename by double clicking to open in a new window. Once the new window is up, you can create any sort of file you prefer be it a reminder, business idea etc. You can also add photos, attachments, and format texts to make it stand out. (Check figure 3 & 4)

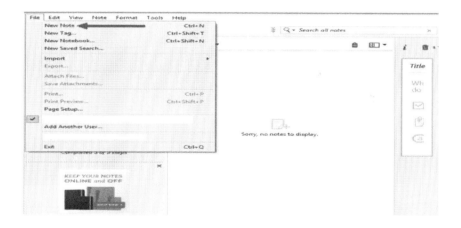

Figure 2

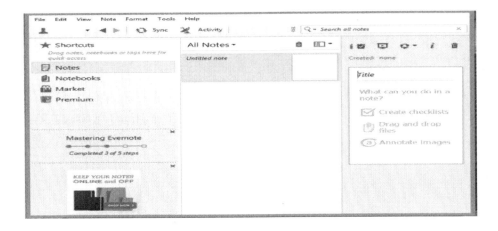

Figure 3

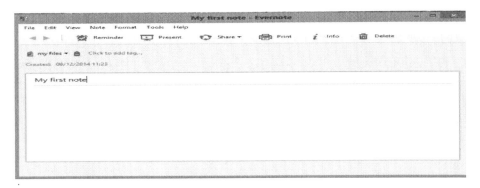

Figure 4

Once you create you first note and give it an appropriate title, go ahead and create some more notes to match any pillar of your life you want to keep organized. You could think of such things like birthday ideas, Christmas gift ideas, New Year resolutions checklist, monthly expenses, daily expenses, etc.

One of the more profound features of Evernote notes is the fact that you can merge two notes into one, tag notes so that you can search and find them easily, use them as

presentations

etc. To merge files, all you have to do is left click the first file, hold CTLR and drag and drop it onto the second file. This is what we call notes merging and it becomes very helpful when you have to merge notes on the same subject. Perhaps I should also mention that once you merge a few files, it creates one single file.

To familiarize yourself with note creation, I suggest you create some more notes, merge them, and get a real feel of the organization that comes with Evernote. This will aid you in developing the Evernote habit of falling into an organizational habit. (Figure 5 below illustrates merging notes while figure 6 illustrates how the file looks after merge)

Figure 5

Figure 6

Now that we have created a few notes, merged, and saved them, did you know that you could also add audios to the notes you create? In fact, you can add a wide array of items to your note or just anything you would add to an email (I have added an image to my note). Just remember that a note cannot exceed 25MB as stated earlier.

In my own view, notes on Evernote simplify the process of keeping ideas, To-do lists, reminders, and all other important notes in one single area. Think of a note as each sticky note you have stuck on your desktop; in many instances, you would want to keep the notes that talk about similar stuff in one place for easy access. It isn't uncommon to even staple some of them together if they have similar ideas that we cannot afford to lose! This is especially useful when you struggle with keeping the napkin notes organized.

You can create a To-do list by using the shortcut keys

CTRL+SHIFT+C or by navigating to your toolbar, and locating the format option. Before we move on from note creation, I should also point out that while creating your notes, if you have any sensitive information, Evernote offers you the option to encrypt some of the data. How? If you have any sensitive text on your notes, you can simply highlight that text, right click and select encrypt now option. This option protects that text with a password, which is crucial when saving sensitive information such as bank account, social security numbers, online passwords etc.

You can create notes using various other methods like:

Click the new note shortcut as shown in the screenshot below then choose the type of note that you want to create. As you can see, you can create a new note, new ink note, new audio note, new webcam note and new screenshot. Each of these has its keyboard shortcut that you can follow with ease if you don't want to waste too much time using the mouse.

The good thing with taking notes is that they sync across all connected devices if connected to the Internet. This simply means that you don't have to worry about forgetting your important notes at work or in a far country after a holiday simply because you can always access your notes wherever you are.

Evernote provides a desktop client, mobile application and web application, making access and retrieval of notes fast and easy. In simple terms, you no longer have to spend hours looking for that napkin you wrote your next big idea on or going through your paper notebook page by page to find that potentially life changing business contact. After creating a few notes, you will realize that they add up fast. This can throw our organizational plan into disarray especially when our notes add up to a few hundred or thousands.

To keep our notes on Evernote properly organized and indexed, the next step is to create a notebook. This is what we shall look at next.

Using Evernote's Notebook Feature

Now that we have created a few notes and saved them in Evernote (you don't actually have to save since evernote does that automatically and syncs the notes across all connected devices every 30 minutes by default), they might cause some form of disarray if you don't arrange them well. I shall explain why. Once you create a note, no matter how many you create, Evernote saves them in a default notebook. This can clutter your Evernote, which if you ask me is contrary to our intention of using the platform. To organize your notes, the team at Evernote advocates that we use notebooks.

What are notebooks? If Evernote is a digital filling cabinet, then notebooks are individual drawers within that filing cabinet. This is an apt comparison with your physical filing cabinet, which you segment to store specific files at specific areas. For example, if you have a physical filing cabinet, you may allocate a drawer of area to sales files, another area to important company files etc.

This is similarly to the Evernote's notebooks. The option to create a notebook is available on the left panel of your Evernote platform (check figure 7a below). If you right click on this option, it should bring up the option to create a new notebook (check figure 7b below).

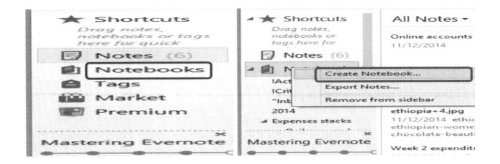

Figure 7

You can also create a notebook by clicking file then new notebook as shown in the figure below.

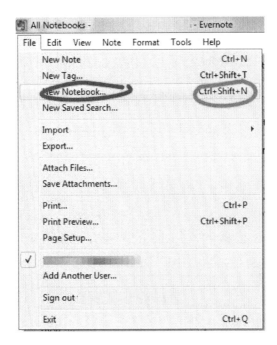

Another handy method of creating a notebook is using Ctrl + Shift + N or clicking on notebooks then new notebook as shown below.

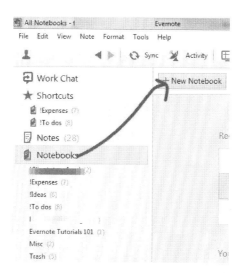

Here is the thing; you can create as many notebooks as you want. In fact, I suggest that you create a new notebook for each pillar of your life, or for notes that contain similar content. For example, if I will create many expenditure notes, ideas notes or even reading notes, then I would create an *expenditure notebook, ideas notebook* and a *reading notebook* just to mention a few. The notebook feature allows you to file notes relevant to each other in one area and thus find them faster than it would take you to go through the default notebook to locate files. I strongly suggest that once you create a note, assign it to a relevant notebook rather than leave it in the uncategorized notebook where it can clutter your Evernote and affect your organization.

Keep in mind that a note can only be in one notebook (just as in real life, a file can only be in one drawer unless of course you have a copy of the same). What does this mean?

It means that if you have an *expenditure notebook* and a *daily expenditure* notebook, you would then have to make a choice of where to place your receipt for that doughnut you bought. To some people, this is restrictive, but it does not need be. As I have said, you can utilize tags to organize your notes and notebooks. In our doughnut example, I may tag the note and the notebook as #expenditure #dailyexpenditure to ensure that it appears in multiple notebooks. Nonetheless, the note will still be in one notebook but the only difference is that you will still access it when you search either of the tags.

Often, I advise Evernote users to create single syllable tags because they are easier to search for in Evernote's search bar. There is no reason why you should make a choice between using notebooks or tags. I have found that a combo of both works better than using one. A notebook can hold many notes (actually, you have up to 100 notebooks to create on Evernote and 100,000 notes to distribute between the 100 notes). After looking at the inner workings of notebooks and their effect on your note organization, let us look at the five key elements to notebook mastery.

A default notebook

As indicated earlier, if you do not specify which notebook to send your notes to, Evernote will automatically stack them in the default notebook. Evernote automatically creates a default notebook from your username. You should change this by

creating a new default notebook or by renaming the default notebook. To ensure that the file appears at the top of the notebook hierarchy, I suggest that you use a special character in your name. Figure 8 shows me creating a "default notebook".

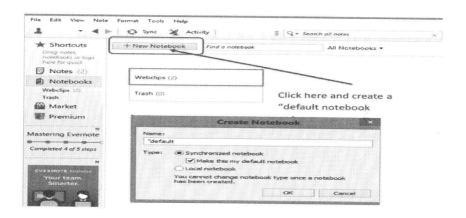

Figure 8

Specified notebooks

As earlier stated, you should strive to create content specific notebooks. Content specific notebooks or specified notebooks are the notebooks you create to house very specific notes. For

17

example, in my Evernote, I have created content specific notebooks in relation to *expenses, reading* and so on. I hope you get idea of what encompasses the creation of a content specific notebook. I have found that creating content specific notebooks is especially helpful in organizing my notes into a systematical organizational structure that makes it extremely easy to find and open notes in an instance.

You should borrow this and carry it on into your Evernote usage. You should create as many content specific notebooks as you require. Figure 9 below shows me creating a @expense notebook.

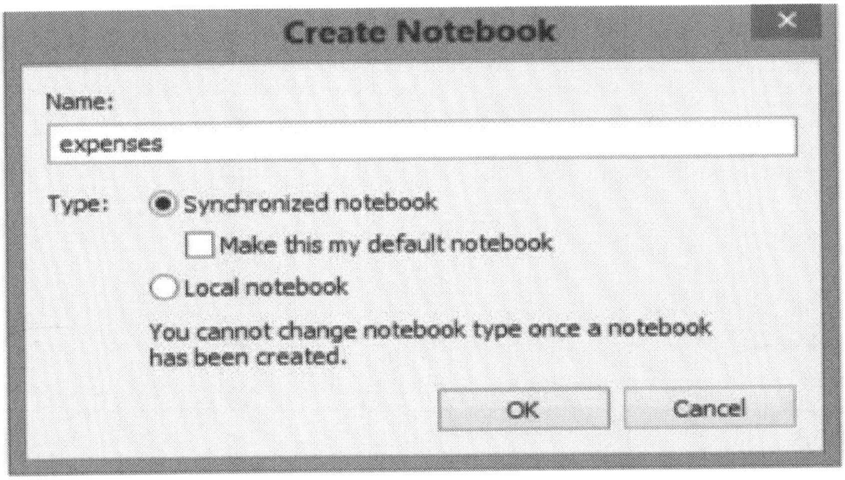

Figure 9

Local or synchronized folder

There is a difference between a synchronized or local folder. A local folder is not available across different devices connected to your Evernote account. This means that the notebook is only available on the device you use to create it. A local folder is ideal for those notes you do not want to synchronize with Evernote's cloud servers. This could be bank information, social security numbers, digital account logins etc. This is useful for those of us who are cybercrime savvy. This is not to mean that Evernote's servers are not secure.

They are. In fact, the team at Evernote guarantees that any information you synchronize with their servers is safe. Nevertheless, taking precautionary measures does not hurt especially with the high rate of cybercrime; in any case, it is better safe than to be sorry.

On the other hand, a synchronized folder is one that synchronizes with Evernote's cloud servers. It is also available across platforms and devices. When you create a synchronized notebook, Evernote automatically synchronizes it with the server at intervals of 30 minutes. However, you can initiate a sync by clicking on the sync button available on your toolbar tools option or by pressing the shortcut key F9. I recommend that you try to use content specific notebooks as often as you can. However, you should note that the free version of Evernote has limited space available i.e. 60Mb. If you want more space, you can upgrade to the premium version of Evernote. Now that we've looked at organizing your notes using notebooks, let us move on.

Supercharge Your Emailing Life

How organized is your emailing life? Do you often find yourself going through a dozen emails to get to the one you need? Do you often find that your email inbox is a chaotic mess of unimportant messages that only serve to distract you as you try to get some work done? Well, you can also use Evernote to supercharge your emailing life. How so? You can do that by forwarding all your important emails to Evernote. This is by far one of my favorite Evernote features. As you can guess, I am very active online. This means I spend a lot of time connecting with friends, making online book purchases, etc. To be honest, almost every part of my life has been digitized even my water bills.

In a world where email spammers vulture around an email address with the aim of making a sale using marketing emails, your inbox can be a dumping ground for emails that have no effect in your life. With this in mind, how many times do you log into your email with the aim of reading an important email only to get side tracked by a very enticing marketing email. Fortunately, you can use Evernote to avoid the hustle of going through your whole email inbox to locate one single but very important file.

By automating and systematizing important email delivery into Evernote, you can stay organized and productive at the same time. This means that if you wish, Evernote could play the role of your traditional email client only better. What this translates to is that you can use Evernote's superior email filtration systems to categorize and organize your emailing life exactly how you want it. Do not take this to mean that you should out rightly ditch your email client!

I am an "email to Evernote" enthusiast. This is especially because it helps me keep my online transactions, travel booking information, purchases, etc. and organizes them in one notebook in Evernote. This helps reduce my stress levels because when all my important emails are in one place in Evernote, I do not find the need to go into my email client to search for a specific email. I can simply use the tag feature in Evernote to fast track my search. Unfortunately, most Evernote users are not aware of the availability of this feature within Evernote. Let us look at how to port emails into Evernote.

Email to Evernote porting guide

You can port emails into Evernote using various methods. However, to keep it simple, we shall concentrate on the simplest method of achieving this.

Step one- Navigate to the tools section of your Evernote application (it is on your toolbar), and select account info.

Here, you will notice a blue colored special email that Evernote assigns you when you sign up. Copy this email to your clipboard. Check out figure 10:

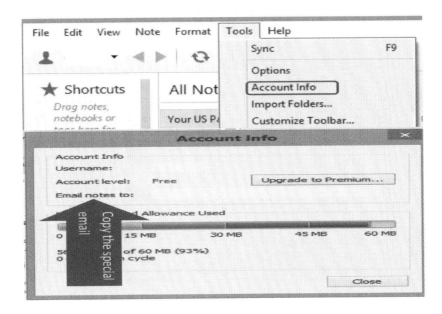

Figure 10

Step two- Step 2 involves adding the special email into our contact list. Log into your email client, find create new contact option, fill in the details, and paste the special email into the contact. After creating the contact, you can choose to forward any important email to Evernote to a specified notebook or into your default notebook. I suggest the former. You should create a specific notebook for all your ported emails to make

sure that they are in one easy to find place. You can also opt to use tags on your email to archive them. To summarize step 2, click tools then options, then go ahead to specify the clip destination, choose the destination notebook then ok! Here is a picture showing just that:

Email delivery automation

On top of porting specific emails into your Evernote, the platform lets you go a step further and automate email delivery straight into your desired Evernote notebook. This is a very precious feature if you want Evernote to replace your default email client. However, I should point out that the process of email automation into Evernote varies with each

email client i.e. automation in Outlook is different from automation in Google mail. Fortunately, with a little help from your search engine, you can easily find your email client automation tutorials online. In our case, we shall concentrate on automation in Outlook mainly because it is one of the most widely used email clients.

Step one- Go to the settings option in your outlook account. (Click the gear icon at the top right hand corner)

Step two- Once here, select options, and navigate to the email forwarding option.

Step three- Select forward your email to another email account and paste your special Evernote email address here. Save and you are done. All your emails will go to Evernote in a notebook of your choice. Here is an illustration of the automation process.

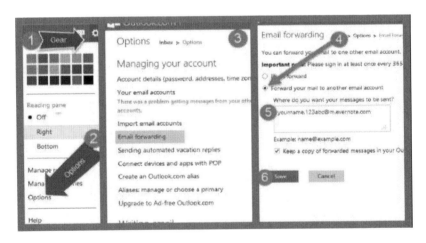

Figure 11

As you can tell, I love Evernote. All the topics we have covered thus far have one aim to make your life easier and less stressful. However, if you are still skeptical about using Evernote, in the next chapter, we shall look at why you should use Evernote before we move on to organizing your physical files by scanning them into Evernote.

Streamline Your Life With Evernote

Have you ever met an unorganized person that lives a stress free life? Organization and streamlining any part of your life directly is dependent on how organized you are. This translates directly into a stress free life. Everything we have looked at so far in relation to Evernote has the sole purpose of organizing all parts of your life in one easy to access place. We have also looked at how to perform all these tasks to make most of your daily note taking easier. Nevertheless, if you are still skeptical about using the application to streamline your life, here are a few more reasons why you must immediately take up its use.

Go paperless

Look around your work desk; how many physical paper files do you see? I would guess many. What if I told you that you could reduce the paper load on your desk by 100%; would that interest you? How would that sound to you? Did you know that you can use Evernote and an app called Cam scanner to scan and store all your paper files as digital files in Evernote? Regardless of which files you want to store digitally, Evernote will store it. You could scan and store reading materials for your course, bank statements, receipts and all other files.

This is very helpful because it reduces the stress of having to search for a file across your desk. With Evernote's notebook creation process we learned earlier, you can create a notebook for all your now digital files. I don't know about you, but for me, less paper clutter is equal to organization, which equals less stress.

Additionally, by signing up for digital copies of your bills delivered to your email, which are automatically delivered to your Evernote notebook, you can reduce your environmental footprint, stay organized, and live a stress free life. In a world fast in shunning anything that has an environmental impact, Evernote paperless feature then becomes the next logical step in going paperless. Actually, you can use Evernote's annotate feature to illustrate anything you want on your scanned documents or digital copies of invoices. Additionally, Evernote uses OCR technology, which means that it is possible to search any text contained in scanned images. Now you don't have to worry about having a hard time searching for receipts or invoices since this feature gives you limitless possibilities in searching for content in your notes.

Ideas on the go

On top of the desktop application, Evernote has a smartphone app. This means that instead of reaching for that paper napkin, you can easily capture notes of those ideas in an easy to arrange and reach place. This means you no longer have to

worry if your napkin notes will be crumpled and become

unreadable. It means that you can write your idea notes on your mobile phone and access them hassle free on your work computer to continue developing them. I have found this to be very helpful especially because brilliant ideas hit us when we least expect it (sometimes while queuing at the bank). Additionally, by developing the idea creation habit in Evernote, you become more creative and productive. Think of Evernote as a digital replacement of your traditional notebook only that when you store files on Evernote, you do not need to worry about carrying your notebook everywhere or freaking out when you cannot find your notebook. Evernote also keeps your ideas safe and secure in one location.

Cloud server's friendly

How would it feel if you lost some very important file? By using Evernote to digitize and store your files, you eliminate the prospect that you might lose files forever. Evernote synchronizes your files with its cloud servers. This is especially helpful when you need to store vital information. By storing your files digitally on their cloud, you can easily access and retrieve the files even if you lose your device. This provides some form of security. The option to synchronize with the server is optional as we saw when we were talking about synchronized or local folders. The server synchronization is useful when you have to store information such as account information, birth certificates, digital copies of your passports etc. The good thing is that you do not have to worry about the security of your files because the cloud servers employ the latest security measures. On the other hand, you can encrypt files you feel contain sensitive information.

Share your notebooks

This is one of my favorite features. After creating notebooks and placing notes in them, Evernote offers you the option of sharing the notebooks with friends or colleagues. This is especially helpful if you are travelling and stumble upon an idea that you would like your team to develop immediately, or have an idea you would like to share with other people and get their opinion. You can share your notes and notebooks on

most social media networks i.e. LinkedIn, Twitter, Facebook, and share your note as an email. With the free version of Evernote, people you share the notebook with cannot edit the file. However, you can add this feature to your Evernote by upgrading to a premium account.

Record meetings

Evernote's create new note function has a record button. The button allows you to create audio recording of meetings, save them and share them with colleagues. This is especially useful in capturing everything discussed in a meeting for future reference. With this option, you can record the meetings and share them with your business partner or have them transcribed, scanned, and stored in your Evernote.

Scan and save documents using Cam Scanner

Despite technological advancements, the development and uptake of portable scanners has been slow. Do you ever wish you could have an easy way to scan documents on the go? Evernote and Cam Scanner are your solution. Cam Scanner is a scanning app that works in conjunction with Evernote to scan and store scanned files directly into Evernote default notebook. To perform this, all you need is a smartphone with a camera, your document, and a flat surface. You then open the application, which activates your camera after which you parse

the camera over the document to scan it; this should upload the document directly to your Evernote account. I have found this feature to be very useful especially in getting rid of document clutter on my desk. Additionally, it is easy and fast to scan documents; it comes in handy when you are not in the office and must scan files. On the other hand, Evernote is also traditional scanner friendly.

Implement Evernote Daily

Capture ideas in images, audio or video

If writing is too tedious, record it in an audio, video or capture a photo to say everything.

Keep a digital library

Instead of keeping hard copies of exams and assignments, scan them and keep copies in your Evernote account. This way, you will reduce clutter and ensure that you never lose any of these documents.

Checklist magic

One of the best ways of ensuring that you track your progress in different activities is to have a checklist. This could also act as a motivator of behavior.

Scan user manuals

If you don't want to get in a situation where you waste too much time trying to locate where you placed a user manual, simply scan it and save it on Evernote; it will be accessible in a click of a button.

Combine penultimate app with Evernote

If you love writing, instead of keeping notes all over, you can simply keep them in one place in your Evernote account. That way, you will be assured that you will never lose such notes.

Collaborate

If you want to streamline project execution, Evernote has a solution for you especially if you are a premium user. First, you can share notes that others can make some comments or edits. You will also be able to chat with those you are collaborating with in the newly introduced chat function.

Recording class notes and business meetings

If it becomes too hard to keep up with the teacher or everyone in a business meeting for you to take notes, record them in audio then revisit the notes later.

Read articles with no disruptions from ads

Use Evernote Cleverly app to make this possible.

Capture holiday ideas and gift ideas

This tool can help you plan your holiday for a long time thus ensuring that you settle for the very best options. As for gift ideas, you can always capture these ideas and keep them nicely organized in your account. You could even capture them in pictures.

Learn a new language

If you don't want to forget how to pronounce words that your friend is teaching you, you can always record them on Evernote. This way, you will be sure of mastering the new language with great ease.

Conclusion

If you want to live a stress free life, the first place to start is organizing your daily workload and chores, which as we have seen, forms the core functionality of using Evernote. However, Evernote is not an organizational magic potion. Even with everything we have learned, regardless of how easy everything is, you still have to put in the time and energy to develop the Evernote habit.

Evernote is the key to the stress free organized life you have been pinning for. By implementing the things we've talked about in this book you can greatly influence the time you spend on tasks every day. Thanks for reading! Now get out there and organize your life.

If you're serious about getting organized and finding more focus in your life be sure to check out my book 'Focus: Sharpen Your Focus, Become Unstoppable and Build Your Dream Life NOW!'

2/9

Made in the USA
Middletown, DE
19 February 2019